D

CARRIE UNDERWOOD

FAMOUS ENTERTAINER

KATIE LAJINESS

BIG BUDDY POP BIOGRAPHIES

Big Buddy Books
An Imprint of Abdo Publishing
abdopublishing.com

abdopublishing.com

Published by Abdo Publishing, a division of ABDO, PO Box 398166, Minneapolis, Minnesota 55439.
Copyright © 2018 by Abdo Consulting Group, Inc. International copyrights reserved in all countries.
No part of this book may be reproduced in any form without written permission from the publisher.
Big Buddy Books™ is a trademark and logo of Abdo Publishing.

Printed in the United States of America, North Mankato, Minnesota.
052017
092017

THIS BOOK CONTAINS
RECYCLED MATERIALS

Cover Photo: Helga Esteb/Shutterstock.com.
Interior Photos: AF archive/Alamy Stock Photo (p. 15); AP Images for Fox (p. 13); ASSOCIATED PRESS
    (pp. 9, 11, 17, 21, 27); Charles Sykes/Invision/AP (p. 25); Danny Moloshok/Invision/AP (p. 5);
    Evan Agostini/Invision/AP (p. 23); Matt Sayles/Invision/AP (p. 29); Tony R. Phipps/Contributor/
    Getty (p. 6); Wade Payne/Invision/AP (p. 19); WENN Ltd/Alamy Stock Photo(p. 15).

Coordinating Series Editor: Tamara L. Britton
Graphic Design: Jenny Christensen

Publisher's Cataloging-in-Publication Data

Names: Lajiness, Katie, author.
Title: Carrie Underwood / by Katie Lajiness.
Description: Minneapolis, MN : Abdo Publishing, 2018. | Series: Big buddy
    pop biographies | Includes bibliographical references and index.
Identifiers: LCCN 2016962365 | ISBN 9781532110641 (lib. bdg.) |
    ISBN 9781680788495 (ebook)
Subjects: LCSH: Underwood, Carrie, 1983- --Juvenile literature. | Country
    musicians--United States--Biography--Juvenile literature. | Singers--United
    States--Biography--Juvenile literature.
Classification: DDC 782.421642092 [B]--dc23
LC record available at http://lccn.loc.gov/2016962365

CONTENTS

SINGING STAR

Carrie Underwood is a famous country singer. She has **released** many albums and won many **awards**.

When she's not singing, Carrie often does **interviews** for magazines and TV shows. She is active on **social media**. There, Carrie shares photos from her personal life.

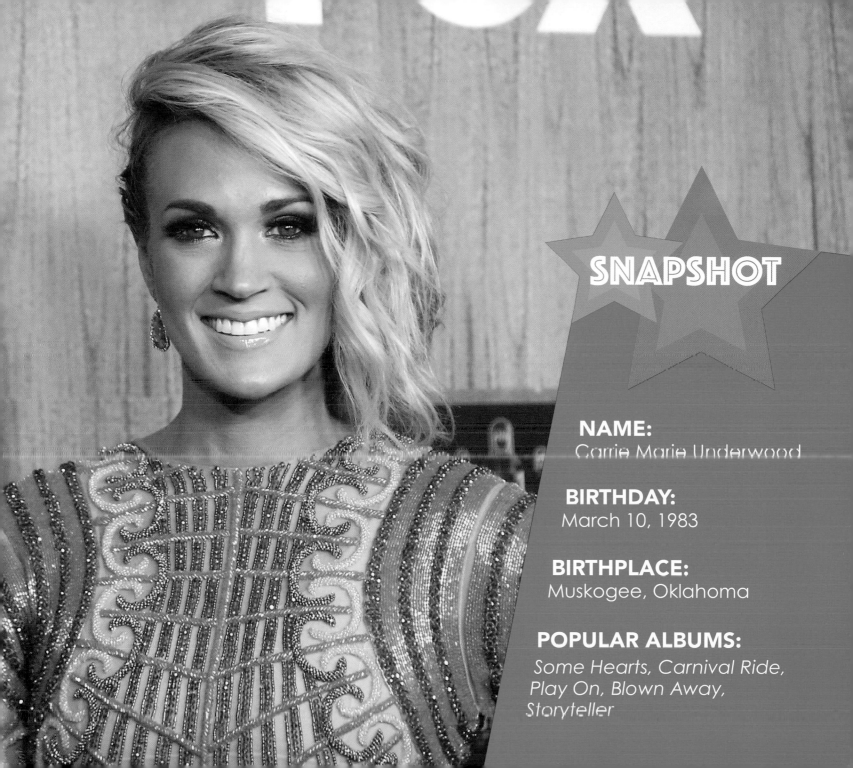

SNAPSHOT

NAME:
Carrie Marie Underwood

BIRTHDAY:
March 10, 1983

BIRTHPLACE:
Muskogee, Oklahoma

POPULAR ALBUMS:
Some Hearts, Carnival Ride, Play On, Blown Away, Storyteller

FAMILY TIES

Carrie Marie Underwood was born in Muskogee, Oklahoma, on March 10, 1983. Her parents are Stephen and Carole Underwood. Carrie has two older sisters, Shanna and Stephanie.

Growing up, Carrie's mother was a teacher. Her father worked in a paper mill.

WHERE IN THE WORLD?

Colorado

Kansas

Missouri

New Mexico

Oklahoma

Muskogee

Arkansas

Texas

Louisiana

MEXICO

GULF OF MEXICO

GROWING UP

At a young age, Carrie began singing in church. She later sang at local events and **performed** in plays. When she was 14, Carrie **auditioned** for a recording company. Sadly, she did not get to make an album.

Carrie graduated from Checotah High School in 2001. Then she went to Northeastern State University. There, she studied mass communication.

Carrie was a good student. In high school and college, she graduated at the top of her class.

BIG BREAK

In 2004, Carrie traveled to Saint Louis, Missouri, to **audition** for *American Idol*. She sang so well, the judges gave her a spot on the show.

In the competition, Carrie sang country music. In May 2005, she became the fourth *American Idol* winner. Carrie won a record contract.

Her first album, *Some Hearts*, sold 8 million copies! It was the top-selling country album of the decade.

About 29 million people watched Carrie win on the *American Idol* finale.

In 2007, Carrie **released** her second album. In its first week, more than 500,000 copies of *Carnival Ride* were sold. "So Small" and "Just a Dream" reached number one on the Billboard Hot Country Songs chart.

In 2009, Carrie made another hit album. *Play On* sold more than 3 million copies. It included songs "Cowboy Casanova" and "Undo It."

DID YOU KNOW
In 2008, Carrie became the youngest singer to join the Grand Ole Opry. She was only 26 years old.

Carrie returned to *American Idol* in 2007. She sang "I'll Stand By You." Her song was downloaded more than 300,000 times.

SUPERSTAR

As a superstar, Carrie was very busy. In 2010, her Play On tour traveled to 50 cities across North America.

Carrie also appeared on major TV shows. She had **roles** in *Sesame Street* and *How I Met Your Mother*.

In 2012, Carrie **released** her fourth album, *Blown Away*. In its first week, the album sold 267,000 copies.

Carrie had a small role in the movie *Soul Surfer*.

In 2012, Carrie took time to sign copies of her album for fans in London, England.

Carrie's success continued. In 2012 and 2013, her Blown Away tour took her to the United Kingdom and Australia.

In 2013, Carrie starred in *The Sound of Music* on live TV. She played Maria von Trapp. The **role** required her to sing and act.

Carrie **released** her fifth album, *Storyteller,* in 2015. It included hit songs "Heartbeat" and "Church Bells."

DID YOU KNOW?
As of 2016, Carrie's record sales topped 58 million.

In 2010, Carrie sang "The Star-Spangled Banner" at the Super Bowl. She also sings the *Sunday Night Football* theme song.

COUNTRY QUEEN

Carrie is known as the queen of country music. Her fans enjoy seeing her **perform** on TV. Since 2008, Carrie and singer Brad Paisley have **hosted** the **Country Music Association Awards**. They are known as a funny and charming team.

Over the years, Carrie has sung many **duets**. She has worked with artists such as Miranda Lambert and Tony Bennett. These songs went on to be big hits.

Carrie and Miranda Lambert (*right*) sang "Somethin' Bad" at the 2014 CMT Music Awards in Nashville.

AWARDS

Carrie has won many **awards**. As of 2016, Carrie has taken home seven **Grammy Awards**. She is only the second country singer to win the Best New Artist award.

Carrie also has won 15 **CMT Music Awards**. This is more than any other artist in the show's history!

In 2016, Carrie accepted the award for Female Vocalist of the Year at the Country Music Awards in Nashville.

ROLE MODEL

Carrie is a positive **role model**. She gives to **charities** to help children, animals, and fighting illness. And, she gives money to help her hometown of Checotah, Oklahoma.

As a **Christian**, Carrie openly talks about her faith. She also sings about religion. "Jesus Take the Wheel" and "Something in the Water" are her most popular Christian songs.

Carrie and Brad Paisley sang at the 2015 County Music Hall of Fame benefit concert.

Fitness is an important part of Carrie's healthy lifestyle. So, she exercises six days a week. Many magazines and TV shows **interview** Carrie about her workouts.

Eating healthy food is important to Carrie. She is a vegan, so she does not eat any animal products.

DID YOU KNOW?
In 2014, Carrie started her fitness clothing line, Calia.

Carrie showed off her Calia fitness line during the 2015 New York Fashion week.

OFF THE STAGE

When Carrie is not **performing**, she spends time with family. In 2010, she married Canadian hockey player Mike Fisher.

Five years later, Carrie and Mike became parents. Isaiah Michael Fisher was born on February 27, 2015.

Carrie has two dogs, Ace and Penny Jean. The whole family lives in Nashville, Tennessee.

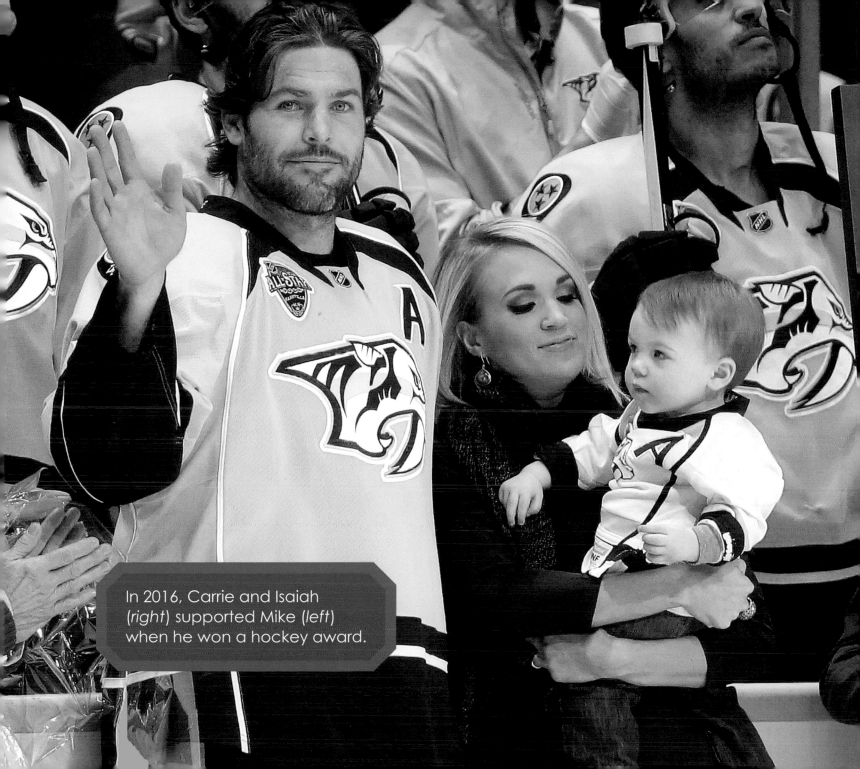

In 2016, Carrie and Isaiah (*right*) supported Mike (*left*) when he won a hockey award.

BUZZ

In 2016, Carrie was on the road for her Storyteller world tour. And, she sang in the United Kingdom, Australia, and New Zealand.

Carrie is the most successful *American Idol* singer. And, she is one of the world's most famous country singers. Fans are excited to see what Carrie does next!

Carrie and Keith Urban sang "The Fighter" at the 2017 Grammy Awards.

GLOSSARY

audition (aw-DIH-shuhn) to give a trial performance showcasing personal talent as a musician, a singer, a dancer, or an actor.

award something that is given in recognition of good work or a good act.

charity a group or a fund that helps people in need.

Christian (KRIHS-chuhn) a person who practices Christianity, which is a religion that follows the teachings of Jesus Christ.

Country Music Association Award any of the awards given each year by the Country Music Association. These awards honor outstanding achievement in the country music industry.

CMT Music Award any of the awards given each year by the Country Music Television station. Winners are chosen by fans who vote online.

duet a song performed by two people.

Grammy Award any of the awards given each year by the National Academy of Recording Arts and Sciences. Grammy Awards honor the year's best accomplishments in music.

host to serve as a host. A person who entertains guests.

interview to ask someone a series of questions.

perform to do something in front of an audience.

release to make available to the public.

role a part an actor plays.

role model a person who other people respect and try to act like.

social media a form of communication on the Internet where people can share information, messages, and videos. It may include blogs and online groups.

WEBSITES

To learn more about Pop Biographies, visit **abdobooklinks.com**. These links are routinely monitored and updated to provide the most current information available.

INDEX